CUSTERIANA MONOGRAPH SERIES

General Custer's Photographers

General Custer's Photographers

By Dr. Lawrence A. Frost

Introduction by
Gregory J. W. Urwin, Ph. D.

Monroe County Library System
Monroe, Michigan

ALL RIGHTS RESERVED TO REPRODUCE OR TRANSLATE

THIS WORK IN ANY FORM OR BY ANY MEDIA

Copyright © 1986 By Lawrence A. Frost

ISBN 0-940696-13-4

*Printed by the
Monroe County Library System
Graphic Services Department
Monroe, Michigan*

CONTENTS

Introduction by Gregory J. W. Urwin, Ph. D. 1

General Custer's Photographers 7

The General's Favorite Photographers 17

Photographers In The West 27

The Little Shadow-Catcher 35

INTRODUCTION

George Armstrong Custer lived from 1839 to 1876, a time when the art of photography was still in its infancy. Yet few figures in American public life have made better use of the camera. During the Civil War, Custer sat for some of the giants of early American photography – Mathew Brady, Alexander Gardner, and Timothy O'Sullivan. Custer's flair for dramatic posturing, his love of garish uniforms, and the genius of his photographers resulted in the most striking series of military portraits produced in the Civil War era.

Custer's Civil War photographs are partially responsible for the fact that his name is as famous today as it was in his lifetime. Authors, editors, producers, and art directors find those images irresistible. They are constantly reproduced in history textbooks, advertisements, documentaries, and books and articles about the West, the Civil War, the Indian Wars, and U. S. military history. Even though Custer was killed eleven years after Appomattox, most publications dealing with his Last Stand are illustrated with a photograph of the "Boy General" who chased glory in the War between the States, rather than the middle-aged

Indian-fighter who encountered defeat and death at the Little Big Horn.

Custer's photographs not only record the peculiarities of his appearance at certain junctures in his eventful life, but they also reveal much about his personality. It is obvious that this man tried very hard to look like a hero. There is no other way to account for the flashy costumes, macho poses, and fierce facial expressions he often adopted when he went before the camera. Even today, military officers recognize that striking the right image can be important in advancing their careers, and soldiers of the nineteenth century were no different. What singled Custer out from so many of his contemporaries was that he not only looked like a hero – he acted like one. He fought bravely and he fought well, and he helped lead the cavalry of the Union Army of the Potomac through a succession of victories in the second half of the Civil War which greatly cheered the war-weary Northern people. These achievements explain why Custer attained high rank and wide renown at such a tender age. They also explain why his fall at the Little Big Horn came as such a shock to the American public, leaving an indelible mark on the nation's consciousness.

Unfortunately, to many modern Americans, particularly those with no knowledge of nineteenth century tastes and standards, the man in the photographs labeled General George Armstrong Custer looks faintly ridiculous. That is the invariable fate of any historical figure who is viewed outside of the context of his times. The blue-coated troopers who followed the "Boy General" into battle and the civilians who thrilled to his exploits in the newspapers did not think he looked ridiculous – but inspiring.

George Armstrong Custer lived in an age when Americans expected their military heroes to dress the part. Cavalrymen especially were supposed to resemble swashbucklers in their conduct and their apparel. While Custer undoubtedly outdid the majority of his peers in this regard, there were many cavalry commanders on both sides in the Civil War who matched him with the colorfulness of their attire. Among them were such flamboyant figures as Turner Ashby, Jeb Stuart, John Hunt Morgan, Nathan Bedford Forrest, John S. Mosby, Heros Von Borcke, and Thomas L. Rosser of the South, along with Hugh Judson Kilpatrick, Alfred T. A. Torbert, Charles E. Capehart, Richard A. Rush, and Alfred N. Duffie of the North.

Those who examine the photographs of the "Boy General" should keep two other things in mind.

First of all, they are looking at a man barely free of his boyhood who is endeavoring as best he can to look older. Custer was only twenty-three when he was elevated to the rank of brigadier general on June 29, 1863. He was twenty-four when he was breveted to major general a little more than a year later. Custer was aware that his youth was a possible detriment to his military career. It could have hampered his efforts to win and retain the confidence of his superiors and subordinates. Therefore, he did his best to appear and act commanding. If he sometimes overdid things, that should not be surprising. Young men are notorious for their extravagance.

Secondly, brigade and division commanders of the Civil War were expected to lead their troops into combat. Soldiers reserved their warmest praise for those officers who got out in front and were the first to brave the enemy's fire. George A. Custer was such a leader. "Our boy general never says, 'Go in men!'" Custer's cavalrymen would brag. "He says, with that whoop and yell of his, 'Come on, boys!' and in we go, you bet." Custer's conspicuous uniform not only made such courage more dangerous and admirable, but it also made him a more effective combat commander. No matter how confusing the situation or thick the gunsmoke, the "Boy General's" troopers always knew where he was. As one of Custer's officers wrote, "That garb, fantastic as at first sight it appeared to be, was to be the distinguishing mark which . . . was to show us where, in the thickest of the fight, we were to seek our leader."

Because the informed reader can glean so much from the study of General Custer's photographs, the Monroe County Library System is to be congratulated for adding this volume to its distinguished Custer Monograph Series. There is another reason for congratulations. The author of this work is the historian best qualified to address the subject of *General Custer's Photographers*.

The "Custer bug" first bit Dr. Lawrence A. Frost at the start of World War II more than forty years ago, and his fascination with America's most controversial soldier has never waned. Indeed, Larry Frost is largely responsible for the current healthy state of Custer studies. His many fine books and articles have exposed thousands to his contagious enthusiasm for the life and times of George A. Custer. Though a podiatrist by profession, Larry molded himself into a capable scholar and amassed what was possibly the best private collection of Custer photographs ever seen in the twentieth century. He single-handedly sparked a renewal of public interest in Custer photographs with the publication of his first major book, *The Custer Album: A Pictorial Biography of General George A. Custer,* in 1964. With the 1984 re-release of *The Custer Album,* followed by D. Mark Katz's 1985 opus, *Custer in Photographs, General Custer's Photographers* is a timely addition to the ever-expanding field of Custeriana. This volume will take its rightful place beside Dr. Frost's other outstanding contributions and stand the test of time as a standard reference for anyone interested in the Custer story.

                      Gregory J. W. Urwin, Ph. D.
                      Department of History
                      University of Central Arkansas

General Custer's Photographers

The year of 1839 marked two events that would leave their effects on American history.

In early 1839 Louis Jacques Maude' Daguerre, a Parisian artist, invented the first photographic process. Later that year, December 5 to be exact, George Armstrong Custer was born in New Rumley, Ohio.

Louis Daguerre accidentally discovered that exposing an iodized silver plate in a camera and then fuming it with a mercury vapor, resulted in an image.[1] By nature a shy individual, he attempted to keep his process secret. The French Government prevailed upon him to allow them to publish the process, a suggestion that became acceptable when he was presented with a large annual pension.

The daguerreotype was a silver-plated copper sheet 6½" x 8½" in size, polished until mirror bright. Placed in a box and exposed to iodine vapors, a thin, yellowish coating formed on this mirrored surface as silver iodide. Following a lengthy exposure in a camera, the plate was placed in another box and subjected to vapors created by heating mercury, forming "an amalgam in proportion to the lights and shades of the original subject."[2] The plate then was washed in sodium hyposulphite, followed by a rinse in distilled water. The results were dramatic, but the process was painful to the sitter for, in bright sunlight, the victim might have to sit motionless for as long as 40 minutes.

Samuel F. B. Morse, of Morse code fame, was the first to bring news of Daguerre's invention and later claimed to be the first to use the process in America, but unknown to him, D. W. Seager had beaten him to it.[3]

Elaborate Establishments

The acceptance of the daguerreotype in America was immediate. At its zenith in the early 1850s, 3,000,000 daguerreotypes were taken annually. Establishments in principal cities were elaborate. A report in a French photographic journal indicated:

"They are palaces worthy of comparison with the enchanted habitations which Orientals erect for their fabulous heroes. Marble, carved in columns or animated by the chisel of the sculptor, richly embroidered draperies, paintings enclosed by sumptuous frames, adorn their walls. On the floor lie rich carpets where the foot falls in silence. Here are gilded cages with birds from every clime, warbling amidst exotic plants whose flowers perfume the air under the softened light of the sun. This is the American studio."[4]

Daguerreotypes were made in many sizes, the 6½" x 8½" being known as the "whole plate" size.[5] The most popular was the one-sixth plate which brought the operator about $5. The price was lowered as the business increased which was assisted immeasurably by the California gold rush of 1849. Prospective miners rushed to obtain daguerreotypes for those they were to leave behind, and in turn, obtain daguerreotypes of their loved ones to take with them. Prices gradually reduced, the one-sixth plate dropping to $2.50.

Daguerreotypes soon were made small to fit into rings and lockets and, conversely, large ones, 15" x 17", were made for the wealthy or extravagant. The latter sold for as much as $50 apiece, the plate costing the operator almost $10. By 1853 some operators advertised daguerreotypes as low as twenty-five cents.

General George Armstrong Custer, ca. 1864, attributed to Mathew Brady.

Brady, Photo Historian

The daguerreotypists with the elaborate studios and high overhead were incensed over the invasion of the "cut-raters." Mathew Brady evidenced this in one of his ads in New York papers:[6]

"Address to the Public — New York abounds with announcements of 25 cent and 50 cent daguerreotypes. But little science, experience, or taste is required to produce these, so-called, cheap pictures. During the several years I have devoted to the Daguerrean Art, it has been my constant labor to perfect and elevate it. The results have been that the prize of excellence has been accorded to my pictures at the World's Fair in London, the Crystal Palace in New York and wherever exhibited on either side of the Atlantic . . . ."

Mathew B. Brady, the photo-historian of the United States of his day, was born in Warren County, New York in 1823 or 1824; no one seems certain which year. His formal education must have been meager since, according to one biographer,[7] "evidence to prove Brady could write was far from impressive."

Brady had been studying photography under Samuel F. B. Morse since 1840, starting in business for himself at Broadway and Fulton Streets in New York in 1844.[8] His first daguerreotypes were superb. A perfectionist by nature, he was tireless, working from dawn until his light source failed. His inherently weak eyes grew weaker from the overwork he willingly imposed upon himself.

Since exposures were long, from 4 to 40 seconds, he constructed in his studio several skylights that were used in conjunction with specially designed reflectors. He was probably the first to use such a method of skylighting.[9]

It was a common practice to use an "immobilizer" (head clamp). Brady had an endless fund of entertaining stories and the ability to tell them well – a trait that served as an analgesic during the travail with the head clamp.[10]

Additional Galleries

The main reason for Brady's success was not his technical ability. From the opening of his first studio he had prevailed upon every celebrity he could reach to "sit" before his camera and "have his likeness made."[11] During his lifetime he photographed practically all of the presidents alive. His photographs of other outstanding personages are without parallel, for he traveled far and wide to photograph statesmen, politicians, authors, scientists or actors.

As his fame grew his business flourished, necessitating the opening of additional galleries. In 1852 he opened one at 205 Broadway; and another in 1853 at 359 Broadway.[12] Brady's Washington Gallery was opened in 1858 in a two-story house on the corner of Pennsylvania Avenue and Seventh Street.[13] For the time being he placed Alexander Gardner in charge, contenting himself with frequent trips to Washington to conduct his business.

In 1860, he opened the most magnificent gallery of all. Within the heart of New York City on the west corner of Broadway and extending along Tenth Street for 150 feet, it was called the National Portrait Gallery. It was outfitted in a costly green velvet carpeting, emerald tinted glass ceiling, luxurious chairs, sofas and divans, and the green walls covered with gold framed examples of Brady's work, many of which were life-size portraits on canvas and finished in oils, crayons or water color.

It was that election year that Abraham Lincoln sat for him, just before his speech at the Cooper Union. And later that year, while New York was agog with the visit of the Prince of Wales, one of the prince's party told Brady that he had his name in his notebook before he had left England, for was he "not THE Mr. Brady who had earned the prize in London nine years ago?" Brady responded by making outstanding pictures of the prince and his party.

Gurney and Fredericks

Although Brady consistently won gold medals at the annual fair of the American Institute of Photography, Jeremiah Gurney of New York, won many important awards during the last years of the daguerreotype era.[14] Gurney began his career in 1840, and in the fifties went into partnership with Charles D. Fredericks, dissolving this partnership in 1856, though both continued in business. Fredericks maintained his business, according to a New York City Directory of 1857, at 585 Broadway.[15] The four-story building was covered with signs advertising his business, the largest in the form of a half circle with cut-out letters over the three upper floors, announcing that this was "Fredericks' Photographic Temple of Art." Above it, and projecting well out from the building, was a replica of a box type daguerreotype camera and lens, on which perched what appears to be an American eagle with wings spread. Next door, a less pretentious building announced "Anson's Daguerreotypes — Large Size for 50 Cents."

Though I have no evidence that George Armstrong Custer ever entered the portals of Gurney or Fredericks', I do have a photograph of Mrs. Custer taken at Fredericks' Knickerbocker Family Portrait Gallery, 770 Broadway, Corner 9th Street, New York.[16]

George A. Custer, ca. 1874, photographed by Eastabrooke.

General's Favorite Photographers

The Custers made frequent use of the military quiet during their winters in the west, to head east for Monroe, Michigan, and then on to more exciting times in New York. This almost annual affair usually meant a keepsake photograph. The General's favorite photographer in the seventies seemed to have been Mora. He was also photographed by another famous New Yorker — Sarony.

Sarony, whose first name was Napoleon, was born in Quebec in 1821, of German parents. The family moved to New York when he was 10. At the age of 12 he was drawing showcards and, by the time he was 21, he had a large lithographic business. By 1858 he was able to retire and devote six years to studying art in Europe. He returned to New York in 1864 to open a photographic gallery at 680 Broadway, and a second establishment in Union Square ten years later.[17]

Sarony was volatile and generous, though eccentric. He successfully sidestepped the conventional pose that was accepted practice and introduced a principle used in art known as "Hogarth's line of beauty." Sarony's great attraction to the theatrical profession assured his success, his art background making him a master retoucher and thereby the friend of all females.

Jose' Maria Mora, a Spaniard born in Cuba in 1849 of wealthy parents, was sent to Europe for an education in art. It was there he became interested in photography. In 1868 his parents left hurriedly for New York to escape the Cuban Revolution. Young Mora followed them. Taking additional photographic training under Sarony, he opened his own gallery at 707 Broadway in 1870. He, like Sarony, specialized in stage celebrities and soon attracted the social set.[18]

His "trademark" was the variety of backgrounds he could use. After several years he had 50 painted backgrounds, which grew to several hundred and made his studio look like the property room of a large theater. A large share of his business was the sale of "publics" which were the cabinet photographs of stage and other celebrities.

Wet Plate Process

Cabinet photographs sold for $12 a dozen; cheaper places making them for $3. The cabinet photograph, introduced in London about 1866, was 4¼" x 6½" with a 4" x 5½" print.

This cabinet size followed the carte-de-visite craze which swept the world in 1857. Because of its small size (2¼" x 4") and low cost, it became a popular substitute for calling cards. Mathew Brady would supply you with several for a dollar. During the Civil War their sales rose to new heights. Soldiers and sailors clamored for them to mail to wives and sweethearts, and vice versa. Brady's staff worked late at night producing thousands of the tiny prints. One photographer (Anthony) recalled making 3,500 in one day.[19]

It might be well to mention at this point that all of this came about with the introduction of the collodion wet plate. The wet plate process was first published by an English architect, Frederick Scott Archer, in March 1851.[20]

The operator prepared his own collodion by mixing equal parts of gun cotton, sulphuric ether and 95 proof alcohol, to which were added the "excitants" — potassium bromide and iodide, or ammonia or cadmium.

Coating the glass plate was a very delicate operation. The prepared collodion was poured on a carefully cleaned glass plate and expertly rolled to the edges to produce an even coating, the surplus being permitted to return to the stock bottle from off one corner of the plate. W. H. Jackson wrote:

"I recall as a small boy, seeing my father coat an 18 x 22 plate. He balanced it carefully on the thumb and fingers of his left hand, poured a pool of collodion in the far, left-hand corner of the plate, and then slowly worked the thick fluid about the edges and all over the plate until it reached the near right-hand corner. So sure and careful was his hand that never a drop was spilled, nor was there any fluid left to be returned to the collodion bottle."[21]

The ether and alcohol was permitted to evaporate to a point that the coating became tacky yet firm. At this point it was lowered into a bath of 60% silver nitrate, remaining there from three to five minutes. Removed, it was placed in a "slide" or "holder" and exposed. Development in the darkroom followed immediately.

Development consisted of pouring on a solution of pyrogallic acid and acetic acid, and then fixing the developed plate in a strong solution of sodium thiosulphate. The time between flowing the collodion on the plate and the development could not exceed eight or ten minutes.

To give you some idea of the exposure times required, in bright sunlight at f/11:

    Original daguerreotype, 1839 — 4,000 seconds
    Bromidized daguerreotype, 1840 — 80 seconds
    Wet collodion plates, 1864 — 8 seconds
    Early dry plate, 1880 — ½ second [22]

The development of a salted paper in 1853 by John A. Whipple of Boston gave a great impetus to the collodion wet plate. The addition of albumin to give the finished print gloss, and the finishing by goldtoning to give it a warm, brown color, were decided improvements.

History Recorded

Until the beginning of the Civil War, Mathew B. Brady's ambition was to make a photographic record of all notables of the period. The war gave him his greatest opportunity to record history with a camera.[23] Receiving permission from President Lincoln and approval of Secretary of War Simon Cameron to proceed if he financed his own venture, he joined General Irvin McDowell in his march on Centreville, Va., July 16, 1861. Brady concentrated on the ravages of war; a documentation of a war-torn existence. When he had finished with destruction and death, he turned to his prewar interests — outstanding personalities. From the sale of pictures of generals and other heroes he was able to help finance his combat photography. His failing eyesight and his inability to be on all fronts at once, forced him to organize teams of photographers. Men like Alexander Gardner (who managed his Washington Gallery through 1862, and later left Brady to establish his own war collection of photographs), Timothy H. O'Sullivan, George M. Barnard, William R. Pywell, James B. Gibson, David Knox. D. B. Woodbury, J. Reekie, Stanley Morrow, H. Moulton, Lewis H. Landy, James Gardner (brother of Alexander), J. B. Coonley, Samuel C. Chester, T. C. Roche, and a Mr. Fox, a Mr. Wood and a Mr. Berger, were members of his team.[24]

Brady's great and immediate need was a mobile camera and darkroom unit. The result was the "Whatiz-zit Wagon" for so it was called by all who saw it. Much like the old horse-drawn butcher's wagon with a step on the rear, and a light-proof door above it, the interior was fitted with bottles of collodion and chemicals, several hundred glass plates, stereoscopic camera, tripods, plate holders, heavy cameras, heavy negative boxes, and a darkroom tent. The wagon was covered with a grayish-white tarpaulin. It took a team of horses to pull all of this.

Brady had two wagons. Ned Hause, his darkroom assistant, would drive one while Brady had Al Waud, artist, and Dick McCormick, newspaper man, ride with him.[25] The tremendous task of setting up equipment, making, exposing, and then immediately developing the wet plates, ofttimes under battle conditions, now seems impossible. How many cameras were damaged and how many plates destroyed either through breakage or improper exposure is unknown. After Appomattox, Brady's entire fortune was exhausted; $100,000 gone and only several thousand negatives no one wanted to buy. In 1873 he filed for bankruptcy but managed to maintain his Pennsylvania Avenue studio in Washington.

Brady Photographs Custer

The first known picture taken of Custer by Brady's staff was a group photograph made at Yorktown by James Gibson in May, 1862. The second is the one of Custer and his old West Point classmate Lt. James B. Washington. According to Horan ("Historian with a Camera") this was taken on Sept. 15, 1862 by Brady.

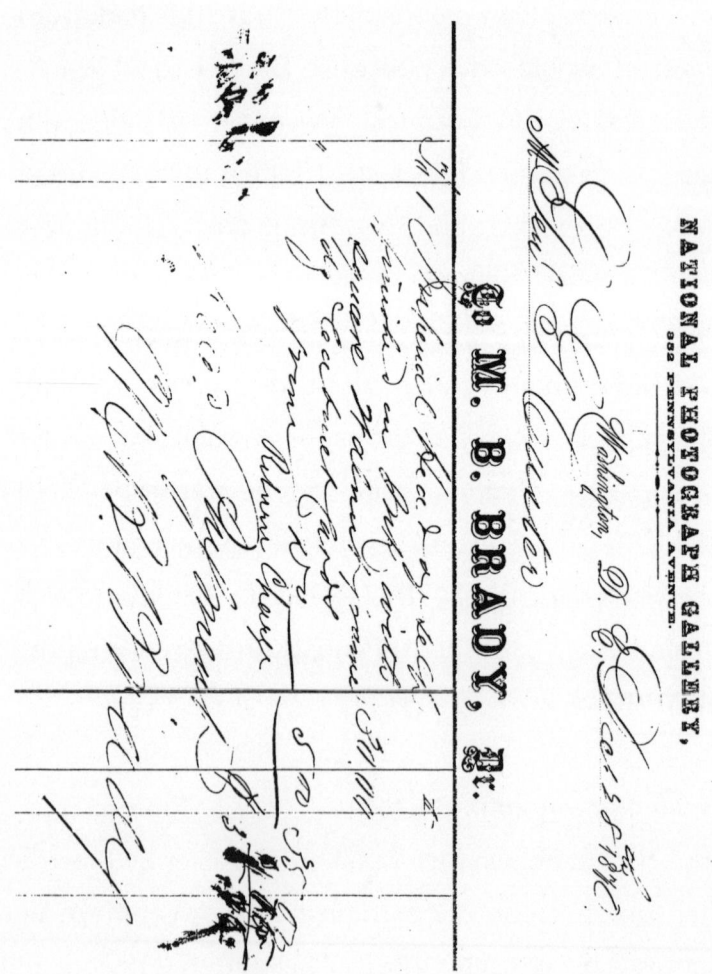

Brady Charges the Cavalry – Dr. L. A. Frost collection.

If so, this was Brady's first occasion to point his lens at Custer. I found an original of this one in Custer's pocket album – about 2" x 3" in size. Later, Alexander Gardner caught Custer when he photographed President Lincoln conferring with General McClellan. That General Custer liked Brady's work is evident by the great number of Custer portraits by Brady in existence. Both the Library of Congress and the National Archives have many, and the Custer Battlefield Museum has others.

I have carte-de-visites of Custer, both as a Brigadier General and a Major General, made by Brady. Brady had a camera for this purpose that had six lenses that took six such photos on one film, all at the same time. These cards had been sent to Custer with the request that he autograph and return them (for sale from Brady's studio). I have seen one other picture of Brigadier General Custer made in Washington by M. J. Powers, a photographer for Jesse H. Whitehurst's Gallery at 434 Pennsylvania Avenue. Whitehurst had galleries in many cities.[26]

I have an original Brady statement sent to General Custer and dated December 28, 1870, for: "one Imperial Head of self finished in ink with square Walnut frame $30.00; one doz-cabinet cards $5.00. Rec'd Payment, /s/ M. B. Brady." This was sent to Custer from the "National Photograph Gallery, 352 Pennsylvania Avenue, Washington." Imperials were enlargements and, as indicated, costly.

Of the portraits I have seen of Custer taken in New York, other than those by Brady, is one by Estabrooke, 31 Union Square. It was taken about 1874, and depicts him as a civilian in a dark suit, ribbon bow tie, a wilted rose in his lapel, and what appears to be a bowler in his hand.

Photographers In the West

An inquiry to the archivist of the United States Military Academy revealed that the first USMA class album to name a photographer was in 1865, which happened to be the Brady Company of New York.[27] Though Mora of New York made Academy class portraits, he did not have his own gallery until 1870. My informant also mentioned (George) Rockwood, 839 Broadway, New York, as having performed similar services for the Academy.[28] Since he was established as early as 1859 it is quite likely he served the Academy for the Class of 1861.

In Monroe, Michigan, Custer's hometown, it has been difficult to obtain information about photographers. The same condition seemed to prevail in other communities. Then as now, photographers kept well in the background, placing all emphasis on subjects before their lens.

It seems highly improbable that Autie Custer had his picture taken in Monroe only twice. When one considers the great amount of time he spent here, and his evident interest in being recorded, one has to conclude that many portraits taken in Monroe have not come to light. I have one photograph of him, a carte-de-visite, showing him as a captain, about 1863, made by William H. Bowlsby. Bowlsby had a furniture store at Monroe and First streets in 1861. When a competitor took up embalming as a sideline, Bowlsby too saw the need for greater service to his community. By 1863 he was established at Front and Washington streets as a photographer, a business he ran through 1867. Monroe had seven photographers from 1863 to 1876 yet, from the available record, Custer entered the door of but the two establishments. It should be noted that a photograph was made by a Bowlsby of General Custer's head-quarters near Winchester, Va., in 1864.[29]

I have several cabinet-size photographs of Custer made by J. G. Hill of 23-25 Front Street. Both are copies of the work of others. The one copy of the Brady favorite of Libbie Custer was made at her request, according to a letter I received from Mr. Hill's daughter. The other is of a portrait made in 1872 in Memphis, Tenn. Mr. Hill opened his Monroe studio in 1878 or 1879, remaining here until 1885.[30]

I have a carte-de-visite portrait of Custer made by Simon Wing when he was in Monroe, 1870-1871.

It would seem natural that Autie Custer would seek photographic luminaries in nearby Toledo and Detroit. A search of their local history files was any empty one.

Alexis Buffalo Hunt

Though the Custers can be followed pictorially, to a slight degree, through the reconstruction period in Texas and his early association with the Seventh U. S. Cavalry in Kansas, no photographers can be identified. It is not until the Grand Duke Alexis of Russia made his trip to America that one can pick up the names of photographers.

General Phil Sheridan had been assigned to take Alexis on a buffalo hunt. In January of 1872, he ordered Custer to leave Elizabethtown, Kentucky, and join him. No order was obeyed more promptly. At the conclusion of the hunt, the entourage headed for Topeka, Kansas, where J. Lee Knight captured the Imperial hunting party on his plate as well as making an exposure of Phil Sheridan and his staff, Custer appearing in both. The date was January 22, 1872.

Jonathan Lee Knight was born in Carroll County, Indiana, and educated at Wabash College. Enlisting as

General George A. Custer, photographed by John A. Scholten, St. Louis, 1872.

a private in the 72nd Indiana Regiment in 1862, he was soon discharged and then commissioned a captain. Mustering out in 1865, Knight moved on to Topeka in 1867, to establish one of the early photographic galleries there.[31]

The ducal party moved on, arriving at St. Louis January 24 where they were showered with attention until the 29th. It was here, apparently, that Alexis and Autie decided upon having pictures taken in their hunting garb. German born John A. Scholten was so honored. He had opened his studio in 1857 after having served a two-year apprenticeship under Andrew J. Fox. Scholten was usually capable, having won numerous prizes for his work. At the 1870 St. Louis Fair he had exhibited every variety of picture from plain photographs, Rembrandts, colored photographs to photographs colored on ivory. His studio, located at 920-922 Olive Street, with nearly 30,000 negatives, was completely destroyed by fire on December 30, 1878.[32]

I have an original Scholten showing Custer leaning on some branches while holding his 50/70 Springfield buffalo gun. Another picture of him in the identical clothing and gun, with the Grand Duke seated to his left, and with the identical props and backdrop, indicates on the back of this original photograph that it was made by Washburn, 113-4th St., Louisville, Ky., and 113 Canal St., New Orleans. Duke Alexis and party arrived in Louisville on January 30, leaving on February 2.[33] Can you arrive at a solution?

The entire group arrived in New Orleans on February 12, having spent February 2 through 8 in Memphis. While in Memphis, Custer had a portrait made by Bingham and Carver, on February 5.

In 1872, Benjamin Bingham and William E. Carver maintained a partnership at 241-243-245 Main Street. By 1876 the partnership apparently had come to an end; though occupying the same address the firm name had changed to "Bingham Brothers."[34]

City Photographers

I have an autographed portrait of Custer in civilian clothes on the face of which he had written "July 1st, 1872" and signed it "Your affectionate brother, G. A. Custer." This cabinet size photo by Scholten of St. Louis, obviously was taken there on the visitation with Alexis for Custer is wearing the same Persian lamb collar worn in the group pictures made at Topeka several days earlier.

Stationed as they were at both Fort Leavenworth and Fort Riley, the Custers made use of the adjacent city photographers. Libbie had a portrait made at S. Meixsell's Gallery of Art in Junction City, Kansas, while they were stationed at Ft. Riley. Autie rode over to Leavenworth City and had E. E. Henry make several views.[35] Nyle Miller advised me that E. E. Henry practiced his art in Leavenworth from 1867 until at least 1882, but nothing is known about him.[36]

During the following year General Custer was ordered with the Seventh Cavalry to accompany General D. S. Stanley and the surveying party for the Northern Pacific Rail Road, known as the Yellowstone Expedition of 1873. A photographer, William R. Pywell, accompanied it. Pywell had served under Brady during the Civil War. The April 15, 1874 issue of the Bismarck *Tribune* contains an ad for William R. Pywell, photographer for the Yellowstone Expedition, in which he indicated that he had his negatives back from the government and could supply prints and stereo photographs. All evidence of his negatives and prints seems to have disappeared. All but one, perhaps. The picture of Custer seated and surrounded by four of his scouts in front of a N.P.R.R. tent is not one of the 55 in the Illingworth series made on the Black Hills Expedition of 1874. It could be a Pywell.

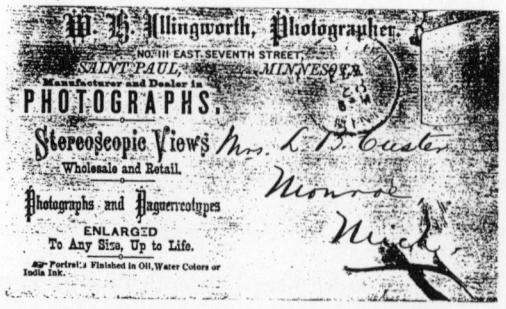

Illingworth – Photographer for Custer's 1874 Black Hills Expedition – Dr. L. A. Frost collection.

The Little Shadow-Catcher

On October 15, 1873, in the Bismarck *Tribune,* Orlando Scott Goff announced the opening of his studio in Bismarck. Goff soon realized that a military reservation offered greater financial reward, bought an interest in the Fort Lincoln Gallery and moved there on November 15, 1873. Undoubtedly many of the photographs in my album, showing the Custer houses at Fort Lincoln, as well as the party pictures and interior groups, were made by him. Though he made many photographs of Indians his greatest achievement was that of making the first photograph of the famous Hunkpapa Sioux chief, Sitting Bull.[37]

Shortly after reestablishing his studio in Bismarck in 1880 — the year the PP of A was founded — he employed David F. Barry and taught him photography, and in 1886 turned his Bismarck gallery over to him. Watson indicated that Barry, in later years, copyrighted and sold as his own many of Goff's pictures, presumably having purchased the negatives.[38]

William H. Illingworth was born in Yorkshire, England, in 1844. He hardly could be called a youngster when he joined the Black Hills Expedition of

General Custer, Black Hills Expedition, 1874. William H. Illingworth photograph.

1874 as its official photographer. His father, a jeweler by trade, had moved to St. Paul in 1850. It was there that young Illingworth learned the jewelers art until he was 20 years of age, then deciding to go to Chicago to study photography. In 1867 he returned to St. Paul, opening up a gallery. That he accompanied the Black Hills Expedition, and that the South Dakota Historical Society has the glass negatives is established. How he happened to be appointed to the position we have not been able to determine though Captain William Ludlow sheds much light on the arrangements:

"A photographer was engaged in Saint Paul, and furnished with a complete apparatus for taking stereoscopic views. He agreed, in consideration of using government material, and being furnished with other facilities, to make six complete sets of pictures upon return to Saint Paul to accompany the official reports. About sixty excellent views (There were but 55 according to Illingworth's printed statement on the back of one of his Stereographs) were taken, illustrating vividly the character of the country. But one incomplete set of pictures was furnished me, which is forwarded herewith. The photographer failed, and subsequently refused, to furnish more, and an attempt to compel him to do so was defeated."[39]

Illingworth retained both his photography gallery and his watch repairing shop in St. Paul until his suicide in 1893.[40] According to C. C. O'Harra, no complete set of his stereographs have been found.[41] The writer has 39 of the original 55 stereographs, part of a set that had belonged to General Custer. And of the 55 stereos, but three had Custer's likeness on them. With them was a photograph of Custer in civilian clothes taken by Illingworth when his gallery was at 97 E. 7th St., St. Paul.

As to his fees, I have a letter from Illingworth addressed to Libbie Custer, from his International Galleries, 111 East Seventh Street, Saint Paul, dated Feb. 27, 1877 in which he advises her he has six cabinets, the price being four dollars.

Which Is the Barry?

Another western photographer of note during the Custer and post-Custer period was David F. Barry. Born at Honecy Falls, New York, on March 6, 1854, and moving to Otsego, Wisconsin, with his Irish parents in 1861, he left no record of his early years there. He learned photography in Columbus, Ohio, at the age of 21 after which he headed for the great west.

Though there are some who disagree; Usher L. Burdick maintains that Barry established a gallery at Fort Lincoln on the west side of the Missouri River in 1875-1876,[42] taking many pictures of General Custer and the Seventh Cavalry. I have not seen evidence to substantiate this in the way of a photograph I could accept, though I know that Barry's name is imprinted on many Custer photographs. Barry was known to do this, and a good example of this custom is Barry's "photograph" of General Custer on page 264 of the November 1929 issue of "The Black Hills Engineer," and also used as a frontispiece by Burdick. I have an identical photo in cabinet size by "Mora" of New York City who was never known to copy and claim another's work.

The Denver Public Library[43] issues a catalog listing 946 Barry photographs of which 15 are of General Custer, three being group pictures. There is no question that Barry was an able photographer who knew and photographed many noted Indians and important officers and civilians. The question to be settled is — Which is the "Barry"? He moved to Fort Buford in

1878, which was 16 miles southeast of the present city of Williston. Barry went Brady one better — he put his portable darkroom in a steamboat. In 1881-1882 he moved to Fort McGinness, and in 1883 moved to Fort Custer for the summer. It was there his portable gallery was destroyed in a storm. Though never having a gallery at Fort Yates, he took many pictures there, too.

"The Little Shadow-Catcher" as he was called by his Indian friends, for he was but five feet high, died at Superior, Wisconsin, August 20, 1932.

I have not determined accurately the actual number of different photographs existent of General Custer though an effort was made to do so. Breaking them down into "portraits" and "groups," one finds them pretty equally divided. The conclusion was borne out by Andrew Loveless, Historian at the Custer Battlefield National Monument, when he advised me that their files indicated 41 photographic portraits, and 41 group photographs that included Custer.[44] The two other major sources of Custer photographs, the Library of Congress and the National Archives, though having a lesser number, seem equally divided in the groups aforementioned. Obviously, there is much duplication of angles, views and groups.

Mr. Loveless cited the difficulty in determining in many cases the date and the name of the photographer. Credits just do not appear on many prints. In the reference Service Report of the National Archives containing views pertaining to General Custer, there are listed 23 portraits, and six groups that include him. Most of these are credited to Brady though Miss May Fawcett, Chief of the Audio-Visual Branch, explains that he had many assistants.[45] In a quick count of the Custer photos in the Library of Congress files, I came up with the number 17. This included my examination of the recently released files of the Handy-Brady Collection in which I found three variations of previously known portraits, and two prints of well-known poses but of much better quality and sharpness.

Unquestionably other pictures of General Custer will come to light from time to time, either as portraits or in groups. But at this point I would estimate there are upward of 100 known photographs. Should any new ones come to light I would appreciate knowing of them.

Of the many accusations hurled at General George Armstrong Custer, none have been that of cowardice. He has never been known to shy away from carbine or bow. Nor could one, following this bit of exploration, accuse him of being camera-shy.

Author's Note

This is a reprint of my article published in the February, March, April and May, 1968 issues of *The Professional Photographer Magazine*. It had been presented before the Chicago Corral of the Westerners and then published in their Brand Book, October 1964 (Vol. XXI, Number Eight) in a slightly longer form that included the footnotes that follow.

SOURCES

1. Beaumont Newhall, **The Daguerroetype in America, New York, 1961, p. 19.**
2. **Beaumont Newhall, Image of America; Early Photography,** 1839-1900, Washington, 1957, p. 1.
3. Ibid.
4. Robert Taft, **Photography and the American Scene,** New York, 1942, p. 76.
5. Ibid, p. 78.
6. Ibid, p. 82.
7. James D.Horan, **Historian With a Camera,** New York, 1955, pp. XIV-XV.
8. Communication from Gilbert A. Cam, Executive assistant, New York Public Library, Aug. 21, 1963.
9. Taft, p. 55.
10. Ibid, p. 32.

11. **Ansconian,** July-August, 1949, p. 1.
12. Horan, p. 20.
13. Roy Meredith, **Mr. Lincoln's Camera Man,** New York, 1946, p. 66.
14. Taft, p. 61.
15. Cam communication; Taft, p. 134 shows a picture of Fredericks Gallery at 585 Broadway about 1857.
16. Communication of A. K. Baragwanath, Curator of Prints, New York City Museum, Aug. 21,1964.
17. Taft, p. 342.
18. Ibid, pp. 349-350.
19. Ibid, p. 22.
20. Edward Epstean, **History of Photography,** New York, 1945. p. 345.
21. William H. Jackson, **Picture Maker of the Old West,** New York 1947, p. VI.
22. Encyclopedia Britannica.
23. Newhall, **Image of America,** p. 3.
24. Meredith, p. 92; Horan, p. 40; Image, p. 3.
25. Meredith, pp. 2-3.
26. Taft, p. 76.
27. Communication of Kenneth W. Rapp, Archivist, United States Military Academy, Sept. 30, 1964.
28. Ibid.
29. Communication of Mrs. E. B. Loughlin, Michigan Section Librarian, Michigan State Library, Lansing, August 27, 1964; and Mrs. Mary Daume, Directory of Monroe County Library System.

30. Communication from Miss Edith M. Hill, Cleveland, Ohio, Sept. 1, 1964.
31. Communication of Nyle Miller, Secretary, Kansas State Historical Society, Aug. 10, 1964.
32. Charles Van Ravenswaay, **The Pioneer Photographers of St. Louis,** Missouri Historical Society Bulletin, October, 1953, p. 69; Communication of Louis M. Nourse, Librarian, St. Louis Public Library, St. Louis, Mo.; Aug. 24, 1964.
33. Communication from Mrs. Dorothy Cullen, Curator and Librarian, The Filson Club, Louisville, Ky., August 27, 1964. Washburn, according to Mrs. Cullen, was a well-known photographer from 1871 through 1881. His association with a New Orleans address is not explained.
34. Communication of Mrs. Violet Hutchenson, Reference Assistant, Memphis Public Library, Memphis, Tenn., Oct. 5, 1964.
35. Communication from Miss May Everhard, Photographer, Leavenworth, Kansas, Sept. 30, 1964.
36. Nyle Miller letter.
37. Elmo Scott Watson, **Orlando Scott Goff, Pioneer Dakota Photographer,** North Dakota History, January-April, 1962, p. 211.
38. Ibid, pp. 214-215.
39. William Ludlow, **Report of a Reconnaissance of the Black Hills of South Dakota Made in the Summer of 1874,** Washington, 1875, p. 8.

40. St. Paul **Daily Globe,** March 18, 1893.
41. Cleopas C. O'Harra, **Custer's Black Hills Expedition of 1874,** The Black Hills Engineer, November, 1929, p. 227.
42. Usher L. Burdick, **David F. Barry's Indian Notes on "The Custer Battle,"** Baltimore, 1949, p. 9.
43. Communication from Mrs. Alys Freeze, Head of Western History Department, Denver Public Library, Sept. 1, 1964.
44. Communication from Andrew M. Loveless, Park Historian, Custer Battlefield National Monument, Crow Agency, Montana, Sept. 9, 1964.
45. May E. Fawcett, Chief of Audio-Visual Branch, National Archives – personal communication.

Custeriana Monograph Series includes the following:

1. *The Life of General Custer*
    by Milton Ronsheim

2. *The Kid*
    by Elizabeth B. Custer

3. *Historical Sketches of General Custer*
    by James H. Kidd

4. *Custer's Last Battle*
    by Richard A. Roberts

5. *Frazier Hunt's Story of General Custer*

6. *Yellowhair*
    by Charles G. Taylor and Jason Kane

7. *The Glory March*
    by Kenneth M. Hammer

8. *Last Statement to Custer*
    by John S. Manion

9. *Witnesses at the Battle of the Little Big Horn*
    by Earle R. Forrest

10. *General Custer's Photographers*
    by Dr. Lawrence A. Frost

*Number Ten
of the Monroe County Library System's
Custeriana Monograph Series*

This is number

199

*of a limited edition
of three hundred.*